Smart Is As Smart Does

Smart Is As Smart Does

Emotional Self Help for Young People

by Sarah McChristian

Proctor Publications

Published in the USA by
Proctor Publications
PO Box 2498
Ann Arbor, MI 48106

Photographs of models Gregory Sizemore and Mikiyo Takemoto
© Paula Christensen Photography.

Library of Congress Catalog Number 97-68827

Cataloging in Publication Data
(Prepared by Quality Books, Inc.)

McChristian, Sarah.
       Smart is as smart does : emotional self help for young
people / Sarah McChristian. -- 1st ed.
       p.cm.
       Includes bibliographical references.
       ISBN: 1-882792-49-1

       1. Adolescent psychology. 2. Self-help techniques for
teenagers. I. Title.

BF724.M33 1997   158'.1'0835
                                  QBI97-40826

This book is dedicated to my Father in heaven
and to all readers who read these words.

Acknowledgments

I want to give credit to the memory of Fonie Butler, a dear teacher and friend. Mr. Butler gave me a great deal of encouragement and was the first teacher to introduce my manuscript to high school students. I want his family, friends, and colleagues to know how much I appreciate his generous concern for my efforts.

Thank you to my spiritual sister, Kathy Jackson, for being my favorite constructive critic. She was my first editor and she remains one of my best friends.

Thank you to my niece, Sharon Bryant-Philips, who is also a teacher. Sharon took me "under her wing" as though I were one of her students. She gave me useful ideas as well as encouraging feedback from her high school English class.

I also want to thank Sharron Russell, staff writer of the *Belleville View* who went "all out" with my first local publication publicity. With coverage like that, Sharron, I was motivated!

Contents

Each of us has an ever-changing, limited emotional capacity for which we have the responsibility to maintain.

Preface

To Parents:

The purpose of this book is to guide the reasoning ability of young people whose minds envision wonderful successes and accomplishments in their futures. It is my intention to assist these young hopefuls in simplifying some *aspects* of the *process* of growing up by providing emotional lessons in *psychological* reasoning. The lessons found herein will provide methods in sound reasoning for focused individuals – those who are keeping their sights upon their goals with the determination to achieve them. These lessons will also aid in providing some direction to those readers who already may have detoured from the paths of their original goals.

Individuals who want to achieve their goals need to know how to keep from *preconditioning* their minds in ways that will be self-defeating. As a song writer cleverly coaxed, we must "accentuate the positive and 'deccentuate' the negative." I hope to show readers how to achieve just that through explanations of some very old lessons in how to *maximize* what is "positive" in life.

It could take many years without these lessons for some individuals to learn these concepts through trial and error. Unfortunately, there are many individuals who may never be skilled in establishing such foundational precepts by which to live. However, the only necessary learning *prerequisites* are a willing heart and a mind that is able to grasp these concepts and use them. These are qualities the reader must already have.

To Young Readers:

We must learn to shift some of the time we engage in random

thinking (reminiscing, daydreaming or just being entertained) to more self-directed or disciplined thinking, which is used in planning, organizing, reading, writing, etc. You ask, but why?

Disciplined thinking helps us achieve the kinds of rewards in life that come from "planning our work and working our plan." It is a fact that successful individuals have the ability to look inward and establish a plan to improve their own personal strengths. Those individuals have also found good reasons to strive to diminish their own personal weaknesses. This kind of exercise in disciplined thinking moves us to higher levels of personal achievement and, thereby, also to higher levels of personal rewards. Successful people *maintain* their emotions, allowing them to *use* their emotions to their benefit.

This short book is a lesson in how to apply emotions. If you learn how to take control of your emotions and not let your emotions take control of you, you will have learned to overcome some of the most *detrimental* barriers that could ever come between you and your future plans. It is my intent to teach you how to use emotions to the best of your advantage.

Note: Words in *italics* can be found in the Glossary on page 36. If many of the words in the Glossary are unfamiliar to the reader, the Vocabulary Exercise on page 39 can be completed prior to reading this book. Young people will receive the additional benefit of learning many useful new words.

Readable Expressions

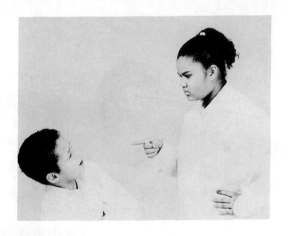

Introduction

"I feel sorry for Tim Murphy," Jeff stated while kicking the pebbles on the ground.

"Yeah, but I'm glad old man Murphy is dead," Jesse replied, holding his head up high as he always did when he felt he had *accomplished* something great. "He really tried to get me in trouble with my old man that time I let the air out of his tires. I'd give anything to see the look on Murphy's face when my old man asked if he expected him to buy him new tires. The man was mean. Mean! I'm sure will be glad to get a new principal!"

"Hey man, Murphy wasn't mean," Jeff argued. "He was just strict. My dad is strict, too, and I get mad sometimes when he's being strict, but I don't hate him for it or wish he was dead!"

Jesse continued throughout the early years of his life believing he was a winner whenever he got his way. He bullied his classmates all through the years in junior high school. One day when Jesse was a sophomore, he *impulsively assaulted* a high school coach, resulting in suspension from school. Jesse became angry at everyone in school and dropped out at age sixteen. He started hanging around with a gang and *subsequently* got into trouble. There was a holdup in which a police officer was killed. The two other guys who were involved said Jesse killed the cop, although Jesse still maintains they are liars.

Back when Jesse was in the first grade, his teachers had been impressed with his reading ability. At that time, Jesse's parents believed he could become anything he wanted to be. His parents now believe they probably gave him a life that was too easy. After Jesse was sentenced and admitted to prison, he was given a variety of *psychological* tests. The prison officials learned Jesse's intelligence was far above average, so they made it possible for him to study electronics.

If Jesse has above average intelligence, would you say that Jesse is smart? Why did Jesse go to prison and his schoolmates did not? What can happen in the life of a young person to cause him or her to choose a *deviant* lifestyle? What is the cause of *faulty* thinking? What kind of psychological controls can a person have so that he or she can *objectively* recognize what the best choices are? Why are some people more reasonable than other people seem to be? Hopefully *Smart Is As Smart Does* will answer these questions for young people and their parents.

Our Equality and Our Emotions

Have you ever wondered why it is said that all men are created equal, when you know that some people are better looking than others? Some people are extremely intelligent while others are learning disabled. Most of us recognize the vast physical and psychological *diversity* that exists among humans. We see that people come in many colors, shapes, and sizes. We know that even identical twins are not exactly alike.

Our *equality* rests in the fact that all of us experience emotions. Emotions are *universal*, which simply means that throughout time, everywhere, humans feel the same *basic* feelings. We all experience the same emotions regardless of the differing *circumstances* that exist in our lives.

Much of what we *accomplish* in life rests upon our emotional state of mind. Our emotions cause us to "move," in other words, to be *motivated*. According to Webster's *New World Dictionary*, the word emotion means "to stir up, having feelings *aroused* to the point of *awareness*." Therefore, we act, we react, and our physical being is acted upon depending on what emotions we have stored within our minds.

Our emotions are remarkably important. Much of the quality of our lives, even how we shape our *destiny*, is determined to a great extent by how we maintain our ever-changing emotional state of mind. In fact, the most *basic* way we define ourselves is through the emotional *process* of comparing ourselves to other people. Generally, people continually rate themselves in comparison to one other.

Although people find less need to compare themselves to others as they get older, this practice is a lifelong process. We shape our *personality* when we *retrieve* emotions from within our minds. Furthermore, we even make friends or enemies based upon the feelings related to the values we have stored within our minds. Whatever basic values we have stored in our minds become the basis from which we compare everything within our *environment,* including people with whom we have contact. We compare all situations and circumstances to the information we have accumulated within our emotional *capacity.*

When we further examine the reasons why people compare themselves to each other, we find that as infants, we begin to compare everything in our surroundings to become familiar with our world. Thereafter, we learn to compare *objects* in our surroundings to establish which objects we appreciate and which objects in our environment we do not like. We continue this process throughout our lives. By the time we become an adult, we have vast *compartments* of stored likes and dislikes in our minds.

Stereotyping

The objects we learn to recognize (the objects established as likes or dislikes) are organized and *imprinted* within our minds. We organize and *categorize* everything. We define this process as "stereotyping" – a means by which we categorize our surroundings to simplify our thought *processes*. By having this ability, which is one aspect of our *defense mechanism*, we do not have to think about all of the things with which we have contact. We can quickly respond to any situation in order to better protect ourselves from harm because we have *compartmentalized* in our minds the ability to determine whether we are in a safe or dangerous setting. Therefore, if we leap three feet away from a curved dark object hidden in tall grass and then recognize the object is a stick, we would already have been out of any danger if the object had been a snake. This system of stored *data* gives us the ability without having to reason, when we are faced with a certain set of *circumstances*, to decide if we should stay and fight or if we should run from what might be a threatening or dangerous situation.

Much of the time, we make good choices – but not always. Sometimes we judge people or situations to be different than they really are. Remember when you were afraid of the dark? Remember when a person, whom you did not like at first, later became a good friend? You discovered he or she was not at all the person you thought they might have been when you first met.

We have many *internal* systems to make us aware of how we feel at any given time. However, the system of stereotyping *enables* us to make choices and categorize data. This system is just as important as any of the other systems we have to *regulate* our physical well-being. We need this ability to reason quickly so that we can quickly respond. The system allows us to *compartmentalize* and store every familiar object in our *environment* into categories within our minds. Our feelings (our emotions) are merely reactions to what is stored within the categories of our minds.

If you were to see smoke curling toward you from under the bathroom door, you would not have to spend time reasoning why you are faced with this unusual situation. Instead, you could immediately respond. You understand from the information you have stored in your mind that this situation is an emergency.

Another useful characteristic of our ability to stereotype allows us to draw from within these categories the sets of values that we have placed on all of the information stored within our minds. We do not have to *analyze* because we already know how we feel about whatever persons or objects happen to be in our surroundings. Thereby, at any given moment, we are aware of whether we like or dislike the kind of setting in which we find ourselves. These likes and dislikes are merely our personal *preferences*. Therefore, we are *preconditioned* to know if we like or dislike certain people, places or objects.

The sets of personal preferences we have stored in our minds determine how we will react to any given situation. How we react to people and situations, to a large degree, determines how successful we are in life because our emotions either free us to make good decisions or *hamper* us from making good choices. There is psychological research suggesting that our ability to control our emotions may be the most *accurate* measure of our intelligence.

During the 1960's, psychologist Walter Mischel began a preschool on the Stanford University campus for the children of faculty and graduate students. Dr. Mischel established a test of self control among four-year-old children. It was called The Marshmallow Test.

Each child was left alone in a room with a single marshmallow upon a table. The adult who left the child alone explained that if the child did not eat the marshmallow, the child would be rewarded with two marshmallows when the adult returned. Some of the children waited and some could not.

Daniel Goleman, author of *Emotional Intelligence*, writes, "Even more surprising, when the tested children were *evaluated* again as they were finishing high school, those who had waited patiently at age four were far superior as students to those who had acted on a *whim*. According to their parents' evaluations, they were more *academically competent*: better able to put their ideas into words, to use and respond to reason, to concentrate to make plans and follow through on them, and more eager to learn."

Society, on the other hand, places the most *emphasis* upon the kind of intelligence defined as the ability to *acquire* and retain knowledge. However, individuals who become successful in life must exhibit qualities other than this typical kind of defined intelligence. Just as important is the fact that we all need to be able to *regulate* our own conduct. The following are the kinds of questions everyone asks him or herself, from time to time, to determine how to best regulate his/her own conduct.

- How can I best motivate myself when faced with *obstacles*?
- How can I control the urges I feel?
- How can I wait for the rewards that I'm working for?
- How can I delay the desire for immediate *gratification*?
- How can I understand the feelings of other human beings?
- How can I maintain the belief that my efforts will make me a better person?

We determine much of the quality of our lives by how we answer these basic life questions. Unfortunately, many of us answer them through an exercise of emotional trial and error. Seldom do we consider the consequences.

Emotional Effects Upon the Body

When we look at other ways in which we are affected by our emotions, we find that scientific research supports the concept that emotions can and do affect us physically. Health professionals involved in medical research continue to report the many physical *ailments* that people suffer due to prolonged overdoses of negative emotions. Such emotions as anger, fear, and worry can be harmful to one's health. Reports from medical personnel state how ulcers, high blood pressure, and hypertension (common results of negative emotions) can be regulated if we change the way we think. On the other hand, if we do not learn to be rid of negative thinking, there are case studies that show it is possible for individuals to become so fearful, they could suffer a heart attack and subsequently die. We can *predispose* our bodies to fail. Cardiologist Bruno Cortis states in *Heart & Soul*, "The mind can effect the heart to the point of creating disease."

If we do not take heed from these kinds of holistic medical and psychological reports, we risk becoming a victim of our own lack of concern about our emotional health. People spend a lot of time practicing ways to stay physically fit, but how often do we exercise the ability we have to maintain our state of emotional well-being? If we don't learn how to "maintain" our emotional state, we could, without even knowing how or when, lose control of our mental *faculties*. The following example is of a patient I encountered at the Northville State Mental Hospital:

> A well-dressed, well-groomed, young mental patient allowed the lemonade from the urn to fill his cup and run over onto the floor. He obviously had lost self-control. Even though the patient's appearance suggested his having had an upper-middle class background, at some point in his life, the young person lost his self-control. He had allowed his

mind to be filled with an overload of negative thoughts. His emotions, and subsequent behavior, become *dominated* by the negative thoughts he never suspected would be so *debilitating* and harmful.

There is a limited number of emotions that our body can withstand before we become ill, either physically or psychologically. Although it cannot be determined what is the limit of negative emotions we must experience before we no longer control our own minds, we recognize this to be the underlying cause of most mental illness. It is *critical* to also understand that we could die from the effects of our very own emotions. We read of individuals who became heart attack victims who were debilitated by extreme fear. Having concluded there is an emotional "limit" to be reached in each of us before we are *adversely* affected in a mental or physical way, it stands to reason there must be an emotional "capacity" within each of us. A capacity is defined as a limited space. Therefore, an emotional capacity is a limited space in which to experience emotions. Now, let's look at the characteristics or *distinguishing* traits of our emotions.

Emotions have always been a part of the human experience. Here is a model of the scale of basic human emotions:

HATE ──────── LOVE ──────── WORSHIP

We will later explain how all emotions relate to and fall within the above range of feelings. First, let's examine how our emotions color our personality.

Disposition, Temperament, and Mood

We have already stated there is a limited number of negative emotions a person can experience before physical or psychological harm occurs. Even those *short-term* negative emotions that may be hardly noticeable continually effect us. We bring about a continual effect upon our bodies by how we use or misuse our emotions. As we establish and store likes and dislikes, this emotional exercise brings about a collection, in our minds, of our own personal choices. Our personal choices are *associated* to our values. We feel strongly about some of our values. Other values, like our feelings, may have less importance to us. It is the constant, moment to moment experience of how we feel about what we prefer that determines our *disposition*. Our disposition can be defined as expressions of our personal preferences. A noticeable change in our disposition (*mood*) can be brought on when we are confronted by anything for which we have extreme negative or positive feelings.

We categorize and store extreme to mild values; we categorize and store extreme to mild emotions. Because we base our actions upon how we feel, and how we feel we base upon what we have stored, it is important that we examine what we store. We *predispose* our behavior by these feelings. These feelings, to a large degree, regulate how we will act in any given situation. How we act and react in situations determines the quality of each situation. Understanding our emotional makeup is the beginning to understanding how to *maximize* our abilities.

Temperament is defined as our usual disposition. However, at times, we discover our stored feelings can be extreme. We may not necessarily exhibit extreme behavior merely because we experience extreme feelings but, whenever we do exhibit extreme behavior, our actions are the direct result of an expression of extreme emotions. These strong feelings not only cause us to "move," in other words, to be motivated, but the strongest of these emotions can cause us to act in ways that can have an *impact* upon our lives. Negative emotions subsequently bring about negative thinking. Negative thinking brings physical and or *psychological* harm to ourselves. The strongest negative emotions could cause us to even strike out against another person. It takes only an instant of emotional *excitation* to trigger ten heartbeats more per minute than what is normal in a state of rest. Once our heartbeat reaches that rate, chemical changes take place within the body that act upon our bodies and minds. Although these chemical changes have to take place to cause us to "move" or act, how we act is not only determined by the extent of the negative emotions we experience, but what *control mechanisms* we have developed. Behavior must be regulated. We all have methods of pushing aside how we feel in order to act appropriately. We will look at the value of pushing aside emotions, in other words *"coping,"* after we examine the relationship between how we feel, think, and act.

Certainly how an individual feels physically affects how that individual acts. The body and the mind are a "two-way street." Therefore, each aspect of our being affects other aspects of our being. We all know it is difficult to project a cheerful mood when we're ill. But we may not be aware of the fact that we are certainly adversely affected physically by experiencing extended periods of negative emotions.

Recently, medical researchers have *associated* chemical changes in the body, brought on by one's emotional state, with the health of one's *immune system*. In *Emotional Intelligence*, Daniel Goleman cites that surgical complications can be caused by the patient experiencing preoperative *anxiety* that, in turn, put the patient at risk for difficulty in recovering as well as at risk of severe bleeding complications. He writes about a study that shows "being *prone* to anger was a stronger *predictor* of dying young than were other risk factors such as smoking, high blood pressure, and high cholesterol."

Other medical records *substantiate* the *insight* that individuals who harbor *toxic* emotions subject themselves to many other ailments. Research scientist Sheldon Cohen found, "the more stress in their lives, the more likely people were to catch cold." On the other hand, surgeon Bernie Siegel in *Love, Medicine, and Miracles* writes, "When we choose to love, healing energy is released in our bodies." Surely there is need for us to examine what we think and how we feel.

When we examine the extreme psychological ailments people suffer, we will discover individuals usually seem to act irresponsibly during the period leading up to their illness. Prior to that point, there are few noticeable behavior changes. It is difficult to establish when an emotional state develops into an emotional disorder, so seldom do we concern ourselves about our own emotional state. Amazingly, most of us lose sight of the fact that if we were subjected to the same prolonged feelings of *anxiety* and *depression* that cause certain individuals to become suicidal or homicidal, we could experience the same psychological problems. We never imagine that what happens to individuals who suffer from extreme anger or fits of *rage* or expressions of violence could ever happen to us. We read about "crimes of *passion*," but we give little thought to how individuals become combative. We like to believe emotional dilemmas happen to other people. We can't imagine ourselves ever being controlled to great extremes by our emotions.

It stands to reason that what can happen to other individuals can happen to us. We all have the physical capability to commit violent acts. It is only necessary for an individual to "move," having been *motivated* by extreme negative feelings to commit a violent act. Therefore, we need to recognize that because the capacity or space in which we experience emotions is limited, our emotions "spill" or "flood" over from our emotional capacity into the areas affecting other parts of our being. Whenever this happens, our negative state of mind may cause us to commit *inappropriate* actions.

Therefore, it seems foolish for us to ignore what we might have stored within our emotional capacity. Let's do what only a few people do. Let's look at what is stored, at various developmental stages, within the emotional capacity of the human species. Then, let's look at how we can examine our own emotional capacity.

Developing Emotional Capacity

Initially, as infants, our emotional expressions are primarily negative. We are *frustrated*, helpless, and dependent. We do not have the ability to understand anything about ourselves or anything about our environment. *Ironically*, the very environment in which we first begin to become aware of our existence is stressful to us. According to Ernst Hilgard and Richard Atkinson, authors of *Introduction to Psychology*, our emotional expressions are subsequently *aroused* by our physical needs for air, food, *elimination*, a comfortable temperature, and sleep. Therefore, with so many needs, it is not surprising that crying is the first human emotional expression. Until we are socialized out of the need to cry, crying proves to be one of the only ways for us, while we are infants, to get our own way. Crying is a natural responsive behavior brought on by an established or imagined fear or threat of something from within the environment. This reactive behavior is natural; one does not have to learn how to cry.

On the other hand, as we gradually establish what is pleasing and therefore acceptable to us, we will be able to laugh. However, we need to be able to experience ideas before we can do so. Although laughing is also responsive behavior, we must have the ability to reason before we can laugh.

Recognizing Values

It takes several years of learning about our environment and language skills to *accurately* communicate how we feel about what is around us. As we grow and become familiar with our environment, we begin to place value on our surroundings at a surprisingly early age. Soon after we are introduced to food, we decide which foods we like. This is when we begin to make choices. Upon learning to *distinguish* one color from another, we select which are our favorite colors. Throughout all of our lifetime, we regularly make choices of personal *preference*. What physical features in others do we find attractive? How do our own faces compare to the other faces we've seen?

We begin to establish a system of personal values when we decide how we want to be treated and then, of course, we must decide how will we treat other people. All the while, these thoughts influence major decisions in our lives about such issues as what kind of person we will marry, how many children we will have, and what kind of house we want. After we examine various people and various lifestyles, we establish an ideal future. We daydream of an existence that may include a wonderful family living in a *thriving* neighborhood of friendly people. Who we initially want to be as adults is planned at some time during *adolescence*. However, throughout our lives, we continually establish values associated with people, personalities, behaviors, dress, and lifestyles.

How will my grades compare to the other student's grades in class? Does my family look and act like most of the other people I know? Is our home as attractive as my friend's home?

Once we have established our own personal set of preferences and values, we begin the task of establishing how we can prepare ourselves to achieve the dreams we have built upon these values.

Changing Values

At an early age in life, many of us may have wanted to be a firefighter. We pictured in our minds how exciting it would be to speed away from the fire station on that enormous fire engine, with sirens blaring, to rescue people and property. Since then, most of us have changed our minds. We have recognized how difficult and dangerous that kind of career can be. Somewhere along the way, we acquired different feelings about wanting to be a firefighter. At some time, with or without being aware of the change, we established different values.

It stands to reason that if we recognize we have the ability to alter the stored categories of "personal preferences" and associated values from time to time, we also can make a *deliberate* effort to change the way we think or feel about anything at any time. The secret here is spending the time and making the effort to promote an improved set of personal preferences. We must examine our emotional capacity and decide which emotions serve us and which emotions do not. For example, is it helpful to me to remain jealous of my best friend? It is beneficial to hold a grudge against my brother? Our next move should be to put forth the effort to rid our minds from such *debilitating* feelings. Only when we learn to "weed out" faulty reasoning can we make room for understanding and acceptance. This exercise in self-awareness gives us a more positive attitude, one that promotes a more positive outlook upon life.

Inside Emotional Capacity

The capacity to experience emotions is limited. This capacity is also in a state of constant change. As a result, today you are a different person than you were yesterday. From the moment of our earliest recollections, each of us have established personal preferences regarding how we feel about everything within our surrounding environment. Furthermore, we react to our surroundings depending upon what we have stored within our emotional capacity.

Now that we are aware that our emotional capacity is limited and our emotions "flow" or "spill" over into the areas of our being that effect us physically and psychologically, we are able to show the concern necessary to protect ourselves from our own emotions. We should desire to examine the condition of our emotional capacity. This capacity is defined as our emotional state of mind. As we have stated, our emotional state of mind – our emotional "makeup" – is a key factor in how we relate to everything and everyone. This emotional capacity is generally filled with a combination of ever-changing positive and negative feelings. However, this capacity can be filled with mostly positive or mostly negative emotions, or any blend of mild or strong feelings.

As an infant, we experienced many negative emotions because we did not have the ability to define the environment. As a child, if we were trained by our caregivers to value ourselves and others, we should be relatively successful in interacting with others. No matter how successful our training may have been, remember we selectively choose our parents' (caregivers') values. Most of our values, however, have been established from our own personal preferences at a time when we were children.

Therefore, we have a need to reexamine the values we established from our personal preferences, established from our likes and dislikes when we were children, if we are to learn how to use our emotions to our advantage.

Emotional Use and Misuse

All *definable* emotions that can be experienced within our emotional capacity are related to the basic emotions of love and hate. The emotions on the negative side of the scale – those related to hate – are anger, sadness, fear, shame, disgust, shock, and other similar feelings. On the positive side of the scale, the emotions related to love are joy, happiness, acceptance, kindness, appreciation, concern, and other similar feelings. The strongest of all feelings is the ability to worship.

The capacity to worship develops only within the individual as he or she becomes mature. That ability is developed when an individual makes more and more of the decisions that shape the direction that individual will take in life. Psychological maturity is defined as the point at which a person moves from the *realm* of being "other directed" to being "self directed." Remember, we create the kind of person we want to be from our personal preferences through reasoning and other complex thought processes. Naturally, we don't always grow up to be the kind of person we want to be. Much of the time when we fall short of our intended goals, it is because, as children, we stored many negative feelings within our emotional capacity, *debilitating* feelings, most often of which we were not necessarily aware. Of course we believed we were justified when we harbored negative feelings; however, these negative feelings are mostly excuses:

- I need to rest.
- I don't have time for that project.
- I can't do that; it's too difficult.
- People might laugh!
- I don't even want to be in the same room with that person!
- I don't have a thing to wear.

Remember when you said some awful words to someone in anger which you never would have said had you not been angry? Whatever set of likes and dislikes you have stored inside your emotional capacity has preconditioned your behavior to any given set of circumstances. This preconditioning determines your disposition. Your disposition colors your personality. *You are what you think.* All of your personal values rest on selected preferences of what you believe is good for you. We all have stored preferences or values about almost everything we consider to be important. These established values are associated with ideas, events, behaviors, appearances, tastes, smells, objects, people, and places.

If we are to function in a way that is most to our advantage, we need to know how to examine what emotions we have stored, especially concerning feelings we have about anything we do not like.

Examining Yourself

When we examine the things we dislike, it should be to determine if we have the power to make those things change. It is foolish for us to dislike anything that we cannot change. We do ourselves a much better service if we accept whatever we do not have the power to change and focus instead upon what we *can* change. To hate war does not stop wars. Wars are a fact that we must accept.

The goal is to *rid* our limited emotional capacity of as many negative feelings as possible. Much hate can be eliminated through understanding the needlessness of hate. In addition, learning not to hate what cannot be changed leads to understanding how to accept the *inevitable*. It is reasonable to accept what we cannot change. Acceptance is a positive emotion. Acceptance is an emotion that is related to love. Once acceptance becomes part of your emotional capacity, it replaces the negative feelings that fill the same space. We now have the ability to feel differently toward a person or situation. Keep in mind that our emotional capacity is an ever-changing, sliding scale. If we have less hate, we can open up more space for love within our emotional capacity and within our lives.

What Goes Wrong

Take a look at the self-defeating behaviors of the individuals briefly described in the following four scenarios and select the extremely negative emotional conduct that most accurately describes the main characters:

A. Low *self-esteem*
B. Fear
C. Hate
D. Anxiety

1. Trudy told one of the other drug counselors that she was sorry she had asked her boss to help her remove the divider that was stuck in her desk drawer. He was a determined sort of person. Without realizing he had been leaning on the drug clinic's silent alarm button, Mr. Brown, with one foot against the side of the desk, continued to exert all the force he could against the divider. When Trudy stepped out into the hall, she ran screaming back into her office. It was too late. She was *critically* wounded by the police officer who responded to the alarm.

2. Three-year-old Patricia was able to sprinkle flower petals all the way down the long church aisle to the altar when the people in the wedding party coaxed her to do so at rehearsal. She had stayed awake all night, however, worrying if she would do a good job the next day at her aunt's wedding. The next day when Patricia saw the church filled with guests, she did not care how many people tried to coax her to walk down the aisle. She would not do it! During the wedding, she sat on her grandfather's lap and fell asleep.

3. A man we'll call Joseph made a major decision while driving home from his high school class reunion. His former classmates

were bankers, doctors, lawyers, and successful business people. He had felt like a failure all evening. He had been working on the same scientific project since his college graduation. When he arrived back at his laboratory, where he also lived, he wrote a brief note and then took his own life. Later, a breakthrough scientific discovery that changed the world of fabrics was found in his laboratory.

4. Fourteen-year-old Benson could no longer tolerate watching his father physically abuse his mother and sister. One evening during an emotional bout, Benson's father repeatedly slapped his mother. Benson reacted and hit his father on the top of his head with the butt of a rifle. Fortunately, Benson's father was not fatally injured.

Answers:
1. B
2. D
3. A
4. C

There is a saying that explains "*hindsight* is 20/20." It is always easier to see with clarity what went wrong after the fact than to prevent things from going wrong. The specific problems young people must overcome relate to how they understand themselves and how each person establishes a path to his or her goals. This involves making the best choices when interacting with others along the way. Every generation has obstacles to overcome. Today, throughout junior and senior high school, the following kinds of perceptions and situations exist.

Ten Existing Common Misconceptions

1. You personally know many students in your class who are experimenting with some form of drugs. Furthermore, you hear about what fun it is to be "high" or "out of your mind." If you don't get high on drugs or alcohol, you remain curious about what you're missing and feel left out.

2. You feel good about yourself only if you are popular. One sure way to be popular is to become sexually active.

3. You notice that the kids who have the most expensive or fashionable clothes as well as the best looking cars seem to have the most fun.

4. The star athletes and cheerleaders know there are kids who would do anything to be their friends.

5. If you study hard and your grades are above average to excellent, most of the other students will feel you are just trying to show off as if you are better than everyone else.

6. If you belong to a particular group, you must not say you disagree with any of that group's activities or beliefs if you want to continue to belong to that group.

7. The more money you have, the more things you can buy. The more things you own, the happier you'll be.

8. The most attractive kids are always the most popular.

9. If you belong to a gang, you will get the protection and respect you deserve.

10. Parents and guardians want to control everything young people do.

Any person who is further along in life beyond the high school years will tell you that the above ideas are <u>all</u> *misconceptions*. Problems arise because many young people believe these misconceptions. The young people who believe and act on one or more of these misconceptions are more likely to be confused and misguided and will often get in trouble. Just remember when you were a child, you did not know about the misery that exists in the world. Now you understand the longer you have lived, the more you understand the nature of misery and what causes it. Let's look at what we can do to make sure we are not surprised by our own behavior.

How to Make Changes

In order to make changes, you must learn about yourself. Cultivate self-awareness. A wonderful tool to help with this is to keep a daily *journal* of situations and events that occur and how you react and feel about them.

The following is an exercise to help you get started. You need a large block of time alone, if possible. Go to the woods or to the beach or anywhere you can relax undisturbed. Sit or lie down and begin to examine the people you know, one by one, beginning with those closest to you. Decide if you have the power to change whatever it is about them you do not like. You will be amazed at how foolish you will begin to feel when you honestly examine if it is reasonable for you to dislike some of the people in your life. Sometimes you may not even know why it is you dislike someone or something. Unless we go through this process, we don't consider that our dislikes are *irrational*! Should you dislike a certain food if that food is good for you? Should you dislike a certain place because it reminds you of a period in history that you hated to study? Should you dislike Aunt Mae because she seems to talk endlessly? Try to remove as many negative feelings (dislikes) as possible. Most people who exercise this ability to "clean house" say they feel relieved of great emotional weight. They can actually feel the difference. Record your experience in your *journal*.

Feelings of hate, anger, fear, anxiety, and similar negative emotions cause chemical changes in the body so that the more often an individual dwells in a state of mind dominated by these types of feelings, the more easily that individual can slip back into the same negative state of mind. The effect is *toxic* to various parts of one's physical and emotional self. Though it is natural for an infant to have a mostly negative emotional state, it is not acceptable for an adult to exhibit fits of anger, outbursts of crying or temper tantrums. Individuals have to learn how to gain control of their emotions to establish acceptable and appropriate behaviors while making the journey from the cradle to the grave.

Most of us are taught we must *cope* with whatever adverse circumstances we do not have the power to change. However, it is emotionally and physically more healthy to learn how to rid ourselves of negative emotions than to strive to cope with whatever is upsetting. To cope with a problem means you must suppress the negative feelings you have concerning the problem. To harbor pent-up emotions as a solution to problems, when practiced over an extended period in one's life, can be detrimental to one's health.

Primary Rule

"Neutral" words are words that are socially polite. If you state you "like" someone, you could truly mean that you love that person or you could possibly be covering up the dislike you feel for them. If you are the speaker, you know what is being expressed. Other times, if you listen carefully to how others express their feelings through speech, you might be given a clue about how they feel when they state they like someone or something. However, most of the time, our true feelings are disguised through the use of *socially* acceptable language. You alone know the truth about how you feel when you speak. Only you can know what is stored within your emotional capacity. But to know yourself completely, you must go through a sincere self-examination process.

If we establish what we mean when we use neutral words such as, "like," "nice," "okay," and similar words, then we can examine the honest meaning behind the feelings being expressed. Only then can we know for sure how we truly feel about all the stored personal preferences within our emotional capacity. We must be completely honest with ourselves during this "cleaning out" process. If we eliminate "neutral" words when we examine how we feel about everything, especially the people with whom we have contact, we can examine our "true" feelings. Determine on which side of the emotional scale each person or thing in your life should be placed – love or hate.

When you find that you do not "like" someone or something, you need to examine the reasons why. If you do not have the power to bring about changes in whomever or whatever you do not like, the question should be, "Why should I *burden* myself with such negative feelings?" To hate unpleasant events, such as severe storms, or creepy crawlers, such as insects, is foolish. Storms are inevitable and insects will always be a vital part of our environment. We must learn to accept the inevitable. Acceptance is a positive emotion. What is also *inevitable* is that in life, we are changing from moment to moment. However, we have the power to change the quality of our lives if we learn to control the kind of information we store within our minds.

Network of Rewards

The more love we have as the *dominant* emotion within our emotional capacity, the easier it is for us to manage with the issues of life. Individuals who understand that negative feelings have an adverse effect upon them, and strive to keep negative feelings at a minimum, are able to maintain an "even" *temperament*. These are the people who are the most successful in life because they have the ability to relate well to a wide range of different (diverse) personalities and situations.

Individuals who exhibit positive reactions to other people and appropriate reactions to most circumstances establish a "network" of persons who are willing to help them meet goals. We all need such a network. We all need friends and people we can contact who can help us achieve our goals or refer us to other people who can help.

However, when our emotional capacity is filled with anger, fear, doubt, etc., we establish few relationships, especially relationships where people want to help us. Furthermore, few people will maintain long standing relationships with those who exhibit more negative than positive emotions. Subsequently, the doors to social and business opportunities are closed to those persons who have "bad" feelings about most events. We all know that type of individual. Although we make suggestions to try to help those kinds of individuals, they usually seem to manage to *reject* our advice.

Avoiding Scars

If we want to prepare ourselves to be the best we can be, we need to reexamine how we feel about people, places, and things with which we have contact. We need to "know" the self within us. This bold step can help us toward the goal of transforming the person we are into a more self-assured individual. Even though the first attempt we make to know ourselves may seem awkward, the effort will certainly be rewarding. We may be surprised to discover the kinds of *debilitating* values we have stored, but most of us would rather be surprised during the *reassessment* process than at some future date by our own negative behavior.

I have yet to meet a prison inmate who, as a child, entertained the thought that any part of his/her life would be spent behind bars. And yet we have controls in our lives to stay out of prison.

Young readers, life's serious mistakes leave scars. Learn about yourselves and make your journeys through life with as few scars as possible. We can correct mistakes, but there is little we can do to take away the scars. We can recover from divorce but those scars will always remain. We could be rehabilitated from criminal behavior, but that record will always be part of our personal history. All of the problems people experience are due to the lack of love they have for themselves and for others. If we love ourselves, we should want others to have what we have.

Our differences should not matter because even though we come from many different backgrounds, we all must learn how to live and we all must learn how to die. Early on, work on discovering your true purpose in life. Learn the best and most beneficial way to live for yourself and for others. Exercise your ability to maintain your emotional capacity with as many positive emotions as possible. This exercise will "clean" the negative emotions from your memory storage and allow more space for love and acceptance. Life will be more rewarding and more fun for you than for those individuals who do not have this understanding. Share this mindset and positive behavior with others whenever you're given the opportunity. Each daily *interaction*, however small and seemingly *insignificant*, can have far-reaching *implications* upon your life as well as upon the lives of those around you.

We must never take our minds for granted. Memory, one aspect of our minds, is often poor, at best. When you compare an event in your memory with the same event on video or film, many details are often lacking. If we add negative emotions to partial or select memories, it is easy to make bad judgments. A partial quote from the book of Proverbs sums up this message: "With all thy getting, get understanding." Try to remember events in your life clearly and learn from your experiences. A not-so-famous but profound quote states, "Use your memory, but don't let your memory use you." You have the power and the ability to develop the life you desire. Examine who you are, cultivate love, and be mindful that your behavior affects everyone around you as you determine the course of your life. Most of all, remember that:

Knowledge + Wisdom = Understanding.

Glossary

academically: scholarly, having to do with general higher education
accomplish: to succeed; to complete a task, time or distance
accurately: carefully; exactly; free from mistakes
acquire: to get or gain by one's efforts
adolescence: the age of a young person (preteen) to adult
adversely: moving or working in the opposite direction; unfavorable or harmful
ailments: any bodily or mental disorders or illness
analyze: to separate (a thing, idea, etc.) into its parts to study or examine the interaction of the inner components
anxiety: the state of being mentally uneasy and worried
aroused: to awaken; to have been stirred into action
aspect: the appearance of something from a specific point
assault: violent attack or unlawful verbal threat
associated: a person or object in the company of another; together
awareness: the state of knowing or realizing; informed
basic: the state of being essential, elementary, absolutely necessary
burden: anything one has to put up with; a heavy load
capacity: the ability or space to absorb, contain or hold
categorize: to put or place into a class or group
circumstance: any happening, fact or event accompanying another condition or factor
compartmentalize: to put in separate compartments, divisions, categories
compartments: separate sections, divided spaces
competent: well qualified, capable, sufficient
control mechanism: the part of a system allowing the ability to regulate or direct actions
cope: to deal with problems or troubles
critical: of or forming a turning point; decisive, dangerous or risky
critically: reasonable judgment determining qualities or faults
data: facts or figures from which conclusions can be made; information
debilitating: to make weak or feeble
defense mechanism: a behavior used to contact or control an encounter
definable: having meaning, boundary or distinguishing characteristics

deliberate: carefully; done on purpose
depression: low feelings, gloominess or sadness
destiny: a seemingly necessary course of events
detrimental: harmful
deviant: turning aside from the normal direction
disposition: the quality of one's emotional state
distinguish: to separate apart; mark off by differences
diversity: the quality of being different, dissimilar, varied
dominate: exercising rule, authority or influence; prevailing
elimination: to remove, take out or get rid of
emphasis: attention or importance given to make something stand out
environment: surroundings affecting the development of its inhabitants
equality: state of being equal or having the same status
evaluate: judgment determining quality or value
excitation: being aroused
faculties: powers of the mind (will, reason, etc.)
faulty: defective, blemished, erroneous or imperfect
frustrated: disappointed; to have no effect; to prevent from having
gratification: state of being pleased or satisfied
hamper: to keep from moving or acting clearly
hindsight: the ability to see after the event
immune system: the means of resisting or protecting from disease
impact: the force of moving against or together
implication: a resulting effect or connection
imprint: early learned associations that establish marked, set behavior
impulsively: sudden human action without thought
inappropriate: not suitable
inevitable: that cannot be avoided; certain to happen
insight: awareness of one's own mental attitude and behavior
insignificant: having no meaning; small; of little or no importance
interaction: to act on or with another
internal: inward; inside
ironical: description of what might be expected to be the opposite
irrational: lacking the power of reason; senseless
journal: a regular written record of events
magnitude: greatness in size or numbers; loud or bright in importance
maximize: to increase to the highest or as much as possible; enlarge
misconception: misunderstanding; interpreted incorrectly

mood: an expressed mental attitude indicating a person's disposition

motivate: to move by some power or force

object: a thing, item, good or ware

objective: a known or perceived goal

objectively: thinking or acting independently, without favor or bias

obstacle: anything that gets in the way; obstruction; hindrance

overwhelming: to make helpless; overpowering

passion: a strong emotion that has an overpowering effect

personality: expressed distinctive patterns or qualities of behavior

precondition: a condition beforehand allowing something else to occur

predictor: something that indicates what will or should happen

predispose: to make receptive beforehand; susceptible

preference: a first choice

prerequisite: required beforehand

process: a method; prepared by special treatment

prone: a natural bent or leaning

psychological: of the mind; mental

rage: madness; furious uncontrolled anger; great force of violence

realm: region, area or place

reassessment: to estimate or determine value more than once

regulate: control, govern, direct or rule

reject: refuse to take, use or believe

retrieve: to get back, rescue, recover or restore

self-esteem: belief in oneself; self-respect

society: group of people regarded as a community

short-term: extending over a short period of time

subsequently: happening secondly as the result of the first occurrence

substantiate: to show to be true or real; to prove

temperament: one's usual frame of mind or natural disposition

thriving: flourishing or successful

toxic: of, affected by or caused by a toxin (a poisonous compound)

universal: occurring everywhere and affecting all things in a group

whim: a sudden fancy, idea or desire

Vocabulary Exercise

Fill in the blanks with the appropriate given words.

I. a. academically   b. accomplish   c. accurately

1. I hope you can —— each task by the end of the day.
2. If you had not been in such a hurry, your math assignment would have been done more ——.
3. The students found junior college to be more —— challenging than trade school had been.

II. a. acquire   b. adolescence   c. adversely

1. Bill's leg injury —— affected his chance to play the game.
2. Each student had to work hard to —— the best possible grade.
3. —— is the time in life for most of us to daydream about our goals.

III. a. ailments   b. analyze   c. anxiety

1. The loud noise at 2 a.m. caused much —— in the minds of the campers.
2. The aged woman had a list of physical —— to discuss with her doctor.
3. You must look at all the pieces of a jigsaw puzzle before you begin to ——— how to put it together.

IV. a. aroused   b. aspect   c. assaulted

1. The smell of dinner cooking can cause your appetite to be ——.
2. The thief —— the store clerk even though he had given him all of the money in the cash register.
3. Every —— of the case had to be examined by the jury.

V. a. associated   b. awareness   c. basic

1. Good health is a —— concern of every school coach because coaches are responsible for the welfare of each team member.

2. The police thought the best friend of the boy they arrested may have been —— to the crime.
3. —— can only be experienced when you know something for sure.

VI.   a. burden   b. capacity   c. categorize

1. A donkey can carry a heavy load, so it is called a beast of ——.
2. To sort means the same as to ——.
3. The —— of the quart bottle is sixteen ounces.

VII.   a. circumstance   b. compartmentalized   c. compartments

1. The —— in the top desk drawer made it convenient to store paper clips and rubber bands.
2. The detective took time to review each —— surrounding the case.
3. The best possible container is —— for each kind of item to be stored.

VIII.   a. competent   b. control mechanism   c. cope

1. A light switch to a light is the same kind of —— that the brain is to the human body.
2. The most —— school counselors are those who know the abilities and needs of the students.
3. Often, children must learn to —— with the younger brothers and sisters who are attracted to their belongings.

IX.   a. critical   b. critically   c. data

1. As soon as all of the —— is gathered, we can determine how much the project will cost.
2. Body temperature above 104 degrees is —— because the subject can suffer brain damage.
3. —— speaking, any parent who cheats on their income tax return does not set a good example for their children.

X.   a. debilitating   b. defense mechanism   c. deliberate

1. The student made sure there were no misspelled words on her paper because she wanted to make a —— effort to get a good grade.

2. The wrestler expanded his chest to the limit, using a natural —— to impress his opponent as he approached the ring.
3. A dose of chemicals from each cigarette is small but has definite —— effect upon the smoker's lungs.

XI. a. definable   b. depression   c. destiny

1. The girl's father had been dead for more than a year, but whenever she thought of him, she would sink into a deep state of ——.
2. The sound of the dog whistle was only —— when it was within the human audible range.
3. A recent saying devised to encourage girls to participate in male-dominated fields is, "biology is not ——."

XII. a. detrimental   b. deviant   c. disposition

1. Lack of sleep can be —— to all parts of your body.
2. Skipping school and hanging out at the arcade was —— behavior for Mark because he had always had more constructive interests.
3. If you overheard someone saying unkind and untrue things about you, your —— would probably change.

XIII. a. distinguish   b. diversity   c. dominate

1. The —— among the people and their customs was more noticeable at the international airport than at most other places in the city.
2. The younger dog was able to —— the old dog in attracting the attention of the owner.
3. A common clue indicating color blindness is when the subject cannot – —— between blue and green.

XIV. a. dominant   b. elimination   c. emphasis

1. The —— of a key soccer player decreased the chances for the team to win.
2. —— is usually placed at the end of a song when the pace of the music is retarded.
3. The team that won has been the —— team in the state for the past three years.

XV. a. environment b. equality c. evaluated

1. Discoveries in science prove particles in the air formed from burning certain fuels affect most of the inhabitants within their ——.
2. People who are concerned want —— for all citizens.
3. Once the circumstances surrounding a problem have been ——, plans can be made to solve the problem.

XVI. a. excitation b. faculties c. faulty

1. The driver placed the blame of brake failure on —— workmanship because the new brake pads had been installed recently.
2. When we lose our internal ability to choose what we will do or what not to do, we have lost control of all of our ——.
3. Recognizable signs of agitation or —— are faster speech rate, higher voice pitch, and rapid eye movement.

XVII. a. frustrated b. gratification c. hamper

1. The strong gusts of wind would either help or —— whoever happened to be serving the volleyball.
2. —— is the state of mind we experience when we acquire something we have wanted and now finally have.
3. However, we become —— when we cannot have what we want.

XVIII. a. hindsight b. immune system c. impact

1. To examine something that has already happened is called ——.
2. The —— of the stone against the car windshield was strong enough to leave a crack.
3. Multiple vitamins can be taken to boost our —— in protecting us from serious illness.

XIX. a. implications b. imprinted c. impulsively

1. Young children have a tendency to behave more —— than adults.
2. Young ducklings are —— within 11 to 18 hours after birth to follow their mother .

3. There may be —— of cheating if several students have the same wrong answers on the test.

XX.   a. inappropriate   b. inevitable   c. insight

1. —— behavior is usually associated with negative consequences.
2. Learning who we are and why we behave the way we do gives us —— into human behavior.
3. It is said the —— consequences of life are death and taxes.

XXI.   a. insignificant   b. interaction   c. internal

1. No matter how —— viruses seem, they can cause serious harm to us.
2. If a telephone's exterior is clear plastic, we can see its —— components.
3. Every person who goes on-line with their computer adds to all the —— that is taking place on the internet.

XXII.   a. ironically   b. irrational   c. journal

1. Some of the ship's crew members kept a daily —— of their voyage.
2. —— the captain felt ill and was unable to write in his daily log.
3. Yelling at the umpire because you disagree with his call is —— behavior.

XXIII.   a. magnitude   b. maximize   c. misconceptions

1. Marsha paid her own expenses for college by working two part-time jobs because she needed to —— her income.
2. —— usually lead to actions that are not appropriate.
3. The church bells were sounded with such ——, they could be heard throughout most of the village.

XXIV.   a. mood   b. motivated   c. objects

1. Jamie was —— to work harder than ever to achieve good grades now that he finally was on the honor roll.
2. The —— of the audience was one of excitement throughout the performance of the high-flying acrobats.
3. The shelves were filled with —— other than books.

XXV. a. objective b. obstacle c. overwhelming

1. The winds were so high, the pilot's main —— was to land safely.
2. The enormous forest fire had an —— effect upon the area wildlife.
3. One —— after another seemed to get in the way of her plans.

XXVI. a. passion b. personality c. precondition

1. The beauty pageant judges searched for a pleasing —— to complement the physical features of each contestant.
2. Careful planning is a —— to success.
3. The finalist had such a —— for the sport, he spent several hours each day practicing.

XXVII. a. predictor b. predisposed c. preference

1. Once you make up your mind, you are —— to how you will act.
2. Wind speed is a —— in determining to classification of a storm.
3. Chocolate is my —— of an ice cream flavor.

XXVIII. a. prerequisite b. process c. processes

1. One of the —— needed to prepare olives before they can be eaten consists of soaking them in a lye solution for at least seven days.
2. A final —— consists of soaking the olives for another seven days in a salt solution.
3. Both of the above curing processes are a —— to making olives edible because the fruit is hard and leathery.

XXIX. a. prone b. psychological c. rage

1. A —— evaluation will be needed to determine if the mental patient must be confined within an institution.
2. The patient would engage in fits of —— for no apparent reason.
3. Children are —— to act very much like the adults they admire.

XXX. a. realm b. reassessment c. regulated

1. The spoiled fruit was removed from the containers, so now it was time

for a —— to determine how much fruit we have left.

2. A pulse can be felt somewhere in the —— of your wrist between your hand and arm.

3. Patrol officers —— how many cars would be allowed in the parking area.

XXXI.   a. reject   b. retrieve   c. rid

1. Her ideas came too late so the group had to —— them.

2. You must first determine if you have a bad habit before you can —— yourself of the behavior.

3. The dog had to swim far to —— the stick thrown into the lake.

XXXII.   a. self-esteem   b. societies   c. subsequently

1. It would be almost impossible for a child to establish high —— if the child had never received praise.

2. —— have always established rules in order to govern people.

3. If at first you don't succeed, you should —— try again.

XXXIII.   a. substantiate   b. temperament   c. thriving

1. The farmers followed all the rules of planting and cultivating so that now all the crops were ——.

2. Mother had an even ——; you always knew how she would react.

3. The police must —— charges before they can arrest someone.

XXXIV.   a. toxic   b. universal   c. whim

1. Her finger was severely swollen because the bee sting had a —— effect upon most of her hand.

2. The volcano had a —— effect upon the weather patterns in a vast region for several years.

3. Theresa realized her decision to buy the silly-looking hat had been just a —— because when she took it out at home, she didn't even like it.

Vocabulary Exercise Answers

I. b. c. a.
II. c. a. b.
III. c. a. b.
IV. a. c. b.
V. c. a. b.
VI. a. c. b.
VII. c. a. b.
VIII. b. a. c.
IX. c. a. b.
X. c. b. a.
XI. b. a. c.
XII. a. b. c.
XIII. b. c. a.
XIV. b. c. a.
XV. a. b. c.
XVI. c. b. a.
XVII. c. b. a.
XVIII. a. c. b.
XIX. c. b. a.
XX. a. c. b.
XXI. a. c. b.
XXII. c. a. b.
XXIII. b. c. a.
XXIV. b. a. c.
XXV. a. c. b.
XXVI. b. c. a.
XXVII. b. a. c.
XXVIII. c. b. a.
XXIX. b. c. a.
XXX. b. a. c.
XXXI. a. c. b.
XXXII. a. b. c.
XXXIII. c. b. a.
XXXIV. a. b. c.

Bibliography

Beck, Joan. *How to Raise a Brighter Child: The Case of Early Learning*. Tridal Press, New York.

Blumenthal, Kahn and Andrews, H. *Justifying Violence: Attitudes of American Men*. Institute for Social Research, University of Michigan, Ann Arbor, Michigan.

Brown, Roger. *Social Psychology*. The Free Press, New York.

Cortis, Bruno. *Heart & Soul: A Psychological & Spiritual Guide to Preventing & Healing Heart Disease*. Pocket Books, New York, 1995.

Gardner, Howard. *Multiple Intelligences: The Theory in Practice*. Basic Books, New York, 1993.

Goleman, Daniel. *Emotional Intelligence*. Bantam Books, New York, 1995.

Graham, Hugh Davis, and Gurr, Ted Robert. *Violence in America: Historical and Comparative Perspectives, A Report to the National Commission on the Causes and Prevention of Violence*. Bantam Books, New York, 1970.

Hilgard, Ernst and Atkinson, Richard. *Introduction to Psychology*. Harcourt Brace & World, New York.

KJV; The Bible. Tyndale House Publishers, Inc. Wheaton, Illinois, and Zondervan Publishing House, Grand Rapids, Michigan.

Martin, Barclay. *Abnormal Psychology*. Holt, Rinehart, and Winston, New York, 1977.

Nevitt, Sanford, Craig Comstock & Associates. *Sanctions for Evil: Sources of Social Destructiveness*. Jossey Bros., Inc., San Francisco, California, 1971.

Siegel, Bernie S. *Love, Medicine, & Miracles: Lessons Learned about Self-Healing from a Surgeon's Experience with Exceptional Patients*. Harper & Row, New York, 1986.

About the Author

Sarah McChristian began her career as a drug counselor of clients who were wards of the Court. She then became a Registered Social Worker in the State of Michigan and has worked in various settings, including state hospitals and prisons. She is a published researcher as well as a noted and dynamic speaker. It is her hope to give young people the opportunity to pave the way to a better future by fully understanding themselves.

Smart Is As Smart Does began as a research paper titled "An Application of Emotions," written twenty years ago by the author. In that paper, emotional capacity was coined "triquo" because this capacity is limited to storing the three major emotions (hate, love, and worship) to which all other emotions correlate. The author did not use the term here, however, because she did not want these concepts to be confused with any other established theory. However, the same concepts have been simplified and condensed within this book specifically for young people.

Order Form

Quantity discounts available:
1 – 9 copies: $12.95 U.S. each (add $2.00 in Canada)
10 – 19 copies receive a 30% discount: $9.07 U.S. each
20 + copies receive a 40% discount: $7.77 U.S. each

Please ship ____ copies of **Smart Is As Smart Does** to:
Name: _____
Address: _____
City: _____ State: _____ Zip: _____

_____ copies at $ _____   per copy = $ _____
Shipping ($2.00 per copy, .50 per each additional copy) $_____
     Total amount enclosed $_____

VISA/MC/AMEX # _____
     Exp. date _____

Or mail check or money order with order form to:
Sarron Corporation
P.O. Box 442
Northville, MI 48167–9117

or call (248) 437–2418 for additional information